MANAGING YOUR
BOSS
IN A CULTURALLY DIVERSE SOCIETY

MANAGING YOUR
BOSS
IN A CULTURALLY DIVERSE SOCIETY

Learn to Lead from Bottom-Up

Africa, Where Do We Go From Here?

LARRY JONES-ESAN

authorHOUSE®

AuthorHouse™ UK
1663 Liberty Drive
Bloomington, IN 47403 USA
www.authorhouse.co.uk
Phone: 0800.197.4150

Published by AuthorHouse   07/06/2017

ISBN: 978-1-4817-7001-9 (sc)

Print information available on the last page.

CONTENTS

PREFACE

Over the past decade, we have witnessed a degree of business globalisation and internationalisation that has increased the need for business people operating across geographies to become both culturally and linguistically aware. Thus, sticking to well-rooted but traditional views of the world does not seem to be an option any longer. As Oliver Wendell Holmes explains, "Greatness is not in where we stand, but in what direction we are moving. We must sail sometimes with the wind and sometimes against it—but sail we must and not drift, nor lie at anchor."

Amongst other consequences, these new global competitive environment has made even more clear that companies and governmental organisations need to review how they operate, their structures, and their cultural foundations and set of beliefs. From a personal perspective, learning, knowledge transfer, and professional development activities are also in need of review and change. Research and experience have taught us that widespread, sustained implementation of new practices in classrooms, principal's offices, and central offices requires a new form of professional development. According to Sparks and Hirsh, this staff development initiative must not only affect the knowledge, attitudes, and practices of teachers, administrators, government workers, officers, or employees, but it must also alter the culture and structure of the organization.

Deep and sustained change/reform depends on many of us, not just the very few who are destined to be extraordinary, most times sitting on top of the ladder.

New leadership skills are needed for problems that do not have easy answers from top or bottom. Geert Hofstede explains in his book "Cultures and Organizations: Software of the Mind", how organisational cultures differ from national cultures, and how they can—sometimes—be managed. These concepts have the potential to be adopted in most organisations where tribal and national diversity exist. Leadership, then, is not about mobilizing others to solve problems for which we already know the answer, but about helping them to confront those problems that have not yet been successfully addressed. Most leaders and managers today are in a world of their own, where top-down leadership is the norm. Likewise, subordinates stay in their own sphere in which they are not able to manage "upwards", in what I describe as the 'Managing-up" syndrome.

Collaborative cultures, which by definition have close relationships, are indeed powerful, but unless they are focusing on the right things, they end up being equally wrong or ineffective.

The more complex society gets to be —and the more it experiences rapid, unpredictable, and nonlinear change impacting organisations and our own perception of the world—, the more sophisticated leadership must become. Complexity means change, and the pace of change is increasing, as James Gleick, the author who introduced the concept of chaos into popular parlance, points out in his work "Faster: The Acceleration of Just About Every-thing (1999)".

This book aims to show that today's leaders and followers face a dilemma: failing to act when the environment is radically changing leads to extinction, yet making quick decisions under conditions of seeming chaos can be equally fatal. Along these lines Robert Sternberg concludes that "The essence of intelligence would seem to be in knowing when to think and act quickly, and knowing when to think and act slowly" If we understand how change affects us better, we will be able to influence (but not to control) it for the better. Different studies equally show that the place where we grew up constrains the way we think, feel, and act.

Suffice to say that most are in existence to leave by order from above and they are either not able to make a contribution to their own development, or just capable to challenge orders simply because of their place of birth.

This book discusses the reality that has been sketched above, and posits that organisations and countries alike that could develop and incorporate to their values system bottom-up management capabilities will be better equipped to deal with the challenges of this fascinating but complex world in the 21st century.

ABOUT THE AUTHOR

Larry Jones-Esan has worked in the education sector for more than 15 years, with commercial experience spanning over three decades. The author has contributed immensely to many corporate organisations and start-ups. He is an Entrepreneur, a Business and Management Consultant, Information Technology Professional, a Certified IT Trainer and a seasoned practitioner.

This book comes from the author's personal experience and his ability to add value to organisation both to those who are leading and to those following. Over the years, his experience in different roles and in organising and facilitating workshops and seminars on many exotics subjects in finance and management coupled with an international exposure in trade mission assignments in different countries, particularly in UAE, Asia and Africa, makes writing this book a real experience.

As part of the top leadership team of the London Academy Business School, he managed both the international office staff and the administration of the Academic Affairs department, coordinating the department's annual performance review, training needs and professional development opportunities.

He developed and implemented a marketing and recruitment plan for international undergraduate, postgraduate students and executive programme for champion of industries, Increasing the number and quality of international applications. He has helped many leaders and followers developed functional skills which lead to improvement in their personal impact and performance

Publications:

His written articles include;

- Private Partnership in Funding University Education
- Emotional Literacy in Education and Adulthood,
- Support for Overseas Student in the UK (SOS), Global Imperative of University Governance
- Learn to Break the Chain of Dependency Syndrome

He has also delivered convocation lectures in a number of universities, and appeared on TV/Radio show and interviews including BBC UK, MBC Mauritius. Ben TV, UK, CNBC New York and NTA, LTV Ikeja, Channels TV in Nigeria to mentioned a few.

Education/Membership:

Larry Jones-Esan is completing a Doctor of Philosophy degree (PhD) in International Business Management at the International School of Management (ISM). He holds a Doctorate of Business Administration (DBA) from ISM/ St John's University.

Along with these, Larry Jones-Esan also holds Postgraduate Degree in Management Studies in the UK, Graduate Certificate in Educational Leadership and Management from RMIT in Melbourne, Australia, PgD in IT in Glasgow, Scotland, PgD in Strategic Business Information Technology in Portsmouth University UK, BSc (Hons) in Product Management from South Bank University in London, UK.

He is a Chartered Manager, Member and fellow of professional bodies including British Computer Society (CITP—BCS), Institute of Health Management (MIHM), Institute of Leadership Management (FinstLM), Member of London Chamber of Commerce and Industries, Institute of Analyst and Programmer (MIAP), Membership of Entrepreneurship Institute of Canada (MEIC), and Member of American Management Association (MAMA).

DEDICATION

I dedicate this book to my wonderful wife Naowarat Jones-Esan Nee Niyom the mother of my Son Theo Clinton Jones-Esan who stabilized my destabilized journey after three broken homes, and who comforted me immensely after the death of my 8 years old daughter Sarah Abigail Jones-Esan who passed away on the 2nd Feb 2000, may her soul rest in peace.

My thanks goes to my eldest son Bright Tope who suffered sleepless nights simply because his room is close to my study. He became my sounding board most nights and week-ends. He proof read the books many times by listening to me reading to him from sleep. Bless him. I also dedicate my work to my children, Richard, Cynthia, Kelvin and Theo.

My biggest thanks goes to Almighty God who spared my life from so many calamities and near misses. May your name be glorified.

EXECUTIVE SUMMARY

A diverse workforce in a society can present the workplace with new opportunities and difficulties. This book discusses practical examples of effectively managing your boss in a multicultural society from a bottom-up approach.

The labour market has branched out in many directions since the 'assembly line homogeneity' that was established as an ideal during industrialism. In today's knowledge society, employees can clock in and out in different time zones, and the workforce is often a mix of people of different age, gender, socio-economic background, race and religion.

Consequently, the workforce is becoming more diverse, and the need to manage and lead through a bottom-up approach has arisen. This need is a challenge for many small, medium and multi-national organisations in societies that operate through a top-down model. With a diverse workplace, everyday communication may be complicated when employees lack a shared understanding of unwritten codes or cultural references. However, a recent trend in management has been to aim to turn these difficulties into advantages strategically.

The author demonstrates significant gains that can be obtained from having a diverse workplace

Larry Jones-Esan

and recommends different approaches to effectively manage diversity in a culturally diverse workforce by understanding how to manage and support your boss from the bottom without losing their trust. The author further explains how companies with a diverse workforce can develop the potential to reach out and grow in a broader market and to attract the best people, across cultural and national boundaries. This book analysis the culture shock phenomenon and cultural conflict in the international business arena and recommend the way forward.

Readers will learn how to manage and lead from bottom-up in a society where top-down leadership is the norms and show how to gain the boss and colleagues trust in the workplace without compromising ethics.

INTRODUCTION

What are the most effective ways to manage your boss, co-workers and customer relationship? How can an establishment, its products and services survive in a highly competitive market? Survival in the corporate environment requires dedication and skills. Multinational companies particularly face the great challenge of creating the right atmosphere for large numbers of employees from different social, economic and political backgrounds to work harmoniously in order to achieve a common goal. Although the boss is expected to provide the network for the workers and the necessary tools to close a deal or get the work done, the maxim 'united we stand; divided we fall' remains crucial to the operations of any organization.

There exists in the corporate world rather unrealistic assumptions and expectations about the very nature of the relationship between the boss and his subordinate. Some experts who have expressed an opinion on this subject matter believe that it is just as important to manage one's relationship with his or her boss as it is to manage subordinates, products, markets and technologies. They emphasize that if the relationship is not cordial, neither managers nor their bosses can perform effectively on the job; therefore the responsibility for maintaining the relationship on an even keel should not, and cannot, rest entirely with the boss.

With clear understanding, it is possible for the subordinate to establish a mutually beneficial working relationship that enhances effective productivity and is characterized by unambiguous mutual expectations. Research has clearly demonstrated that personality conflict is only a part—sometimes a very small part—of the problem. More often, the subordinate is oblivious of the fact that his relationship with the boss involves *mutual dependence between two fallible human beings*. Failing to recognize this crucial fact, the staffs typically either avoids trying to manage his or her relationship with the boss or manages it ineffectively.

This problem is accentuated by an erroneous perception of the boss as a "superman" who is capable of carrying on without any significant input from his subordinates. Viewing the issue through this prism, a significant number of staffs fail to appreciate how much the boss needs their help and cooperation to do their jobs effectively. They do not realize that the boss could be severely hurt by their actions, and craves their cooperation, dependability and honesty.

At the other end of the scale are those who see themselves as not very dependent on their bosses. They rarely take into cognizance how much help and information they need from the boss to facilitate the effective performance of their own jobs. This superficial view is particularly damaging in a setting where a staff's job and decisions crucially affect other outcomes in the organization.

A staff's immediate boss could play a critical role in linking the staff to the rest of the organization by making sure that the individual's priorities are consistent with organizational needs, and in securing the resources which they needs to perform well. Yet some staff tends to see themselves as practically self-sufficient, and not needing the critical information and resources a boss could supply.

It would be presumptuous for a staff to imagine that the boss should always know what information or help to render to a subordinate and be always willing to provide them accordingly. Certainly, some bosses do an excellent job of caring for their subordinates in this way, but for a staff to expect *that* from all bosses is dangerously unrealistic. A more reasonable expectation for staffs to have is that modest help will be forthcoming, since bosses are only human. Effective workers accept this fact and assume primary responsibility for their own careers and development. They seize the initiative in seeking the information and help that they need to do a job rather than wait for their bosses to provide them.

Although a superior-subordinate relationship is one of mutual dependence, it is also one in which the subordinate is typically more dependent on the boss than the other way round. This dependence inevitably results in the subordinate feeling a certain degree of frustration—sometimes anger—when his or her actions or options are constrained by the boss' decisions. This is a normal phenomenon in life and occurs in the best of relationships. A staff's success in handling these frustrations largely depends on his or her predisposition toward dependency on authority figures. Under these circumstances, some individuals react instinctively by resenting the boss's authority or rebelling against his decisions. Often, mountains are made out of mole-hills and little conflicts are escalated beyond what is appropriate. The subordinate sees his boss as an institutional enemy, and subconsciously develops a somewhat irrational relationship that seeks to fight him just for the fun of fighting. The subordinate's reactions to being constrained are usually strong and sometimes impulsive. The boss is seen as a spoil-sport who delights in hindering progress, or an obstacle to be circumvented or tolerated. Psychologists refer to this pattern of reactions as *counter-dependent behaviour.*

At the other extreme are subordinates who suppress their anger and behave in a compliant fashion even when the boss makes what they consider to be a poor decision. They would agree with the boss even when a disagreement might be welcome or when the boss might willingly alter his decision if provided with more information or superior argument. Because they bear little relationship to the prevailing situation, their responses are as much an over-reaction as those of counter-dependent managers. Instead of regarding the boss as an enemy, these ones go to the opposite extreme of denying their anger and frustration while tending to see the boss as an omniscient parent who knows best and who should take responsibility for the staff's career, train him in all he needs to know, and protect him from overly ambitious peers. Both counter-dependence and over dependence lead managers to hold unrealistic views of what a boss is. Both points of view largely ignore the fact that most bosses, like everyone else, are imperfect and fallible. They don't have unlimited time, encyclopedic knowledge or extrasensory perception; nor are they evil enemies. They have their own pressures and concerns which are sometimes at odds with the wishes of the subordinate—and often for good reason.

Chapter One

MANAGING YOUR BOSS
IN A CULTURALLY DIVERSE SOCIETY

"An empowered organization is one in which the individual has the knowledge, skill, desire, and opportunity to personally succeed in a way that leads to collective organizational success"—Stephen R. Covey.

Managing your boss and leading others in a culturally diverse society deals with elements such as attitudes, desires, beliefs and customs of people regardless of their geographical locations in today's' business environment. The management, employees and customers are the success triangle of any business. The word "diversity" refers to the way in which people differ from one another. Since such differences affect the way in which people interact in the workplace, diversity management is crucial for most organizations. Managing diversity is a comprehensive managerial process for developing an environment that works for all employees. It is an inclusive process since all employees belong to a culture. It must not be viewed as a sort of

1

us-*versus*-them problem to be confronted but rather as a resource to be managed. In this regard, cultural diversity in the workplace mirrors many of the same issues at play in the realm of international business. Cultural norms shift relative to language, technological expectations, social organization, authority conception, non-verbal behaviour, and the perception of time.

In other words, what is right in one culture is not necessarily wrong in another culture but only different. Cultural diversity often throws up the question of how to manage those varying cultural norms within a single nation. Cultural diversity, as an issue in the workplace, may deal with any differences among people who work together. A broad definition of diversity can have a positive or negative effect on how an organization approaches the issue. On the negative side, as a word, "diversity" is often the subject of debate. Perhaps one of the most promising benefits of cultural diversity in the workplace is the opportunity which it provides for cross-cultural synergy. Synergy—the result of a combination in which the whole is greater than the sum of its parts—has long been a side-benefit or by-product of global business involving multiple cultures.

People differ from one another in many ways, their differences often resolving around individual and cultural traits. These traits and characteristics make an employee unique. These include age, marital status, ethnic background, physical make-up, native language, religion, social class, customs, habits and values. A worker must manage his or her behaviour and job with utmost professionalism. People from different professional and cultural backgrounds make up the total workforce of many organizations to contribute their diverse experience and contact for growth and development. They might have a contact or similar experience that could take the company forward or backward. Often a crucial element is the effectiveness of the communication system within the organization as well as the cooperation and coordination that arise from it.

In order for an establishment to grow and survive, the personnel must be adequately equipped intellectually and psychologically. The employees can only manage their boss if they are provided with ample opportunity to feel a sense of belonging. While the boss may control the pay cheque of the employee, it is the duty and responsibility of the workers to initiate innovative and transformative ideas capable of increasing the company's turn-over, since the boss cannot do it alone.

Creativity Brings Innovation

Even more important than a healthy capital base, the sustainability of a business heavily depends on creative innovation. Business executives must not be afraid of taking a calculated risk in the area of positive change. In this connection, an atmosphere must be created to enable the employees to contribute innovative ideas. The employee, on his part, must seize the opportunity to make an impact. Effectively managing one's boss presents an added advantage: the employee's visibility in proffering useful ideas might prove a personal insurance policy against a possible future lay-off. Besides, the employee may thus be inadvertently acquiring important managerial and entrepreneurial skills as well as contributing in keeping the company afloat. It is difficult to dispense with the services of an employee who is helping the company in maintaining a healthy balance sheet, an employee who virtually doubles as an internal consultant. It all boils down to a willingness or disposition to take the initiative.

An internal consultant may close a juicy deal, write a successful proposal, present ideas that yield money or proffer advice that saves the company from making a bad investment. It was the 19th century American steel mogul and philanthropist, Andrew Carnegie, who said: "No person will make a great business who wants to do it all himself or get all the credit."

In 1991, the State of Massachusetts, U.S.A., was struggling with a $460 million budget deficit. Governor William Weld, who refused to raise more taxes, was considering massive job cuts and reductions in programmes for low-income people. However, mother of two, Kathleen Betts, 38, who for 10 years had been processing medical bills on behalf of the state's Medicaid patients, decided to take the initiative to assist the government in dealing with the dilemma. Through diligent study of Medicaid manuals and Department of Human Health and Services guidelines, Betts uncovered an error in the way in which state and federal establishments calculated hospital operating costs and incomes. It was clear that Massachusetts Medicaid programme was being reimbursed far less than it was entitled to. To correct the problem, the federal government provided an additional $489 million. Declaring that "often the best ideas come from the people on the front lines", Governor Weld sponsored and ensured the passage of a bill that provided a cash reward of $10,000 to Betts and subsequently to state government employees whose initiatives helped government to be more productive.

Realizing that all success arises from daring to begin, the internal consultant constantly seeks for avenues to contribute towards the progress of the organization. He is confident that his ideas and opinions would not be turned down by his boss, and that he was hired to contribute to the realization of the organization's goals and objectives. He sees his boss as human and feels free to discuss a business plan. He does not allow his cultural background to work as a limiting factor against him. He is assertive, maintains a complementary rather than a confrontational relationship with his co-workers, and is a team-player. Since the company is paramount, the internal consultant always maintains a cordial relationship with his boss, fellow employees and the customers.

It is important to remember that cultural peculiarities play a significant role in the behaviour of employees in the workplace. For example, Asian Indians may be reluctant to speak frankly to superiors, while Asians and most Nigerians would rather avoid eye contact as a sign of respect and courtesy. Africans and Britons may break eye contact and turn their heads away in order to concentrate on listening. Some cultures avoid confronting co-workers or contradicting the ideas of superiors no matter how outrageous these might be. On the other hand, Hispanics may feel that contradicting the boss is not disrespectful. Not everyone in an organization is likely to feel at home with the idea of cultural diversity. As a rule, people tend to be more comfortable with others who look, talk like or share affinity in many areas with them. Emphasizing diversity, therefore, might undermine that comfort level.

Since diversity tends to engender new approaches to old practices and long-standing tendencies, some individuals in organizations may find such change troubling. For example, individuals with strong prejudices against certain groups may find rapidly changing demographics in the workforce threatening either because they find change itself disquieting or because they hold a position which they feel they might lose if groups historically excluded from their workplace were allowed to compete in an unhindered way for their positions. It is in order to facilitate diversity in the workplace that, in the United States, Title VII of the Civil Rights Act of 1964 makes it unlawful to discriminate against anyone on the basis of race, colour, national origin or religion.

In all situations, it is the obligation of the worker to manage his boss in spite of diverse cultural influences in the workplace. The workforce run the business but success comes from the customers because they can put a company out of business if they are not happy with its goods or services. It would then be quite easy for a rival company to lure them with a new brand or product. The bottom line for the worker is to keep his boss (and, by extension, himself) in business in the face of competitors, and ensure customer satisfaction. After all, providing goods and services in a satisfying manner remains the principal raison d'être, and the greatest impetus for success, of any business.

In 2004, the Federal Inland Revenue Service, Nigeria's foremost government revenue collection agency, instituted a series of reforms the purpose of which was principally to radically increase the collection of revenue as a result of numerous measures that provided the incentives for voluntary compliance among taxpayers. *"The Taxpayer is King"* was adopted as the mantra for the exercise. Within a period of eight years, the results were amazing. From a modest collection of N1.19 trillion in 2004 to a whopping total of N4.63 trillion was collected in 2011, representing an increase of about 389 per cent.

You can manage your boss when you can think like your boss without stereotyping him or her with just his location on the planet. The managers or the leaders should foster unity and oneness among co-workers. He should assist in raising the level of team spirit and galvanize the individual beliefs, philosophies and capabilities to take the company to the next level. In summary, the staffs manage the managers, customers and the competitors.

"Think of managing change as an adventure. It tests your skills and abilities. It brings forth talent that may have been dormant. Change is also a training ground for leadership. When we think of leaders, we remember times of change, innovation and conflict. Leadership is often about shaping a new way of life. To do that, you must advance change, take risks and accept responsibility for making change happen."—Charles Rice.

Chapter Two

BOSSES ARE ONLY HUMAN, AFTER ALL

"There is no contest between the company that buys the grudging compliance of its workforce and the company that enjoys the enterprising participation of its employees."
—Ricardo Sempler

Owing to the tremendous difference in our perception of, and reaction towards, various issues with which we are confronted, human beings are the most complex species to relate with. Indeed, our perception of reality constitutes the core of our individual human experiences. This truth is clearly illustrated in the story of the six blind men who attempted to use their sense of touch to understand the structure of an elephant. While the one who felt one of the elephant's legs declared to his colleagues that the elephant was like a tree, the one who grabbed the animal's tail insisted that the elephant was like a snake. In the end, they ended up with six different descriptions of the large animal, each of which dealt with only a part of it but failed woefully to create an accurate picture of the object of inquiry.

A great degree of managerial skill is required to coordinate and blend a large number of people from a vast array of socio-economic backgrounds into an efficient and effective team in a workplace. The boss is saddled with the enormous responsibility of dealing with the pressures of the work environment and ensuring that everybody contributes their quota to the success of the organization. To facilitate successful performance, the boss deserves respect and cooperation from his subordinates but certainly not fear. It is wrong and counter-productive for employees to be afraid of their employers. Fear is often a result of a domineering attitude on the part of the boss and is capable of causing the affected staff to always distance themselves from him, thereby creating a relationship gap that could hinder the smooth operation of the organization.

Open communication channels between the boss and the employees enhance the generation of ideas and creative innovations. Potentially useful ideas may occur to the employee but if the channels for passing them to the boss are blocked, they may remain suppressed and never see the light of day. The employees should be allowed a relatively easy access to the boss either to warn him about a project or proffer ideas that could turn to money. The power of the mind and brain must not be underestimated; as soon as a boss observed that he is being avoided by an employee, he should take immediate steps to talk him out of it.

Consider the following anecdote: *The boss is never wrong. If I think he is wrong, I must have made a mistake. If I haven't made a mistake, I must have caused the boss to make a mistake. Even if he is wrong, he is not wrong if he does not admit that he is wrong. If I still think he is wrong after he has admitted no such thing, I am making a mistake—a really big one. The boss is never wrong; this is the one thing that is always right.*

Managing your boss requires that you gain an understanding of both the boss and his context as well as your own situation and needs. Most managers understand this to some extent but many are not thorough enough. At a minimum, the employee should appreciate his boss's goals and pressures, as well as his strengths and weaknesses. What are your boss's organizational and personal objectives, and what are the pressures on him, especially those from his boss and others at his level? What are his long suits and blind spots? What is preferred style of working? Does he like to receive information through memos, formal meetings, or phone calls? Does your boss thrive on conflict or does he try to minimize it?

A top-notch marketing manager with a superior performance record was hired into a company as a vice-president to straighten out the marketing and sales problems. The company, which was having financial difficulties, had been recently acquired by a larger corporation. The president was eager to turn it around, and so gave the new vice-president free rein—at least initially. Based on previous experience, the new vice-president correctly diagnosed that greater market share was required and that strong product management was important in bringing that about. As a result, the vice-president made a number of pricing decisions aimed at increasing high-volume business. When margins declined and the financial situation did not improve, however, the president increased pressure on the new vice-president. Believing that the situation would eventually correct itself as the company gained back market share, the vice-president resisted the pressure.

However, by the second quarter margins and profits had still failed to improve, and the president was compelled to take direct control over all pricing decisions. All items were placed on a set level of margin, regardless of volume. The new vice-president began to be shut out by the president, and their relationship deteriorated. In fact the vice-president found the president's behaviour bizarre. Unfortunately, the president's new pricing scheme also failed to increase margins, and by the fourth quarter, both the president and the vice-president were fired. What the vice-president had not known until it was too late was that improving marketing and sales was only *one* of the president's goals. The most immediate goad had been to make the company more profitable quickly. Also, the vice-president did not realize that the boss had invested in this short-term priority for personal as well as business reasons. The president had been a strong advocate of the acquisition within the parent company, and the boss's personal credibility was at stake.

The vice-president was a victim of several errors. Taking information at face value, he made assumptions in certain areas despite inadequate information, and—most damaging—never actively tried to clarify what the boss's objectives were. Unfortunately, he ended up taking actions that were actually at odds with the president's priorities and objectives. Managers who work effectively with their bosses do not behave in this way. They seek out information about the boss's boss and others around him to test their assumptions. They pay attention to clues in the boss's behaviour. Although it is imperative that they do this when they begin working with a new boss, effective managers also continue to do this because they recognize that priorities and concerns change.

Strengths, Weaknesses and Work Style

Being sensitive to a boss's work style can be crucial especially when the boss is new. For example, a new president who is organized and formal in his approach replaced someone who was informal and intuitive. The new president worked best with written reports and also preferred formal meetings with set agendas. One of the division managers recognized this tendency and worked with the new president to identify the kinds and frequency of information and reports which the president wanted. This manager also made a point of sending background information and brief agendas for their discussions. The manager found that, with this type of preparation, their meetings were very useful. With adequate preparation, the new boss was even more effective at brain-storming problems than his more informal and intuitive predecessor had been.

By contrast, another division manager never fully understood the new boss's work style, objecting to its excessive control. As a result, the manager seldom sent the new president the necessary background information, and the president never felt fully prepared for meetings with the manager. In fact, the president routinely spent quite some time whenever they met trying to obtain fact which should have been supplied beforehand. These meetings proved inefficient and frustrating for the boss, and the subordinate was often thrown off guard by questions that the president would ask. Ultimately, this division manager resigned. The difference between the two divisions managers just described was not so much one of ability or even adaptability. Rather, the difference was that one of them was more sensitive to the boss's work style than the other.

The boss is only half of the relationship; you are the other half, as well as the part over which you have more direct control. Therefore, developing an effective working relationship required that you know your own needs, strengths and weaknesses, and personal style.

Your Own Style

No one is expected to change either his basic personality traits or those of his boss. But you can become aware of what it is about you that impedes or facilitates working with your boss and, with that awareness, take actions capable of making the relationship more effective. A certain manager and his superior ran into problems whenever they disagreed. The boss's typical response was to harden and assert his position, forcing the manager to raise the ante and intensify the force of his argument. In doing this, he would usually channel his frustration into sharpening his attacks on the logical fallacies of his boss's assumptions. His boss, in turn, would become even more implacable about holding his original position. Predictably, this escalating cycle resulted in the subordinate avoiding, whenever possible, any topic having a potential for conflict with his boss.

In discussing this problem with his friends, the manager discovered that his reaction to problem was typical of how he generally reacted to counter-argument—but with a slight difference. His response would overwhelm his friends, but not his boss. Since his attempts to discuss this problem with his boss were unsuccessful, he concluded that the only way to change the situation was to control his own instinctive reaction. Subsequently, whenever the two reached an impasse, he would check his own impatience and suggest that they break up, analyze the issue thoroughly and then come together again. Usually, when they renewed their discussion, they would have digested their differences and become more able to work them through.

Gaining this level of self-awareness and acting on it are difficult but not impossible. For example, by reflecting over his past experiences, a young manager learned that he was not very good at dealing with difficult and emotional issues where people were involved. Because he disliked those issues and realized that his instinctive responses to them were seldom good, he developed a habit of finding a way to connect with his boss whenever such a problem arose. Their discussions always produced ideas and approaches which the manager had not considered. In many instances, they also identified specific actions which the boss could take to help.

Dependence on Authority Figures

Although a superior-subordinate relationship is one of mutual dependence, it is also one in which the subordinate is typically more dependent on the boss than the other way around. This dependence inevitably results in the subordinate feeling a certain degree of frustration, sometimes anger, when his or her actions or options are constrained by the boss's decisions. This is a normal part of life and occurs in the best of relationships in different society. The way in which an employees or managers handles these frustrations largely depends on his or her predisposition toward dependence on authority figures.

Some people's instinctive reaction under these circumstances is to resent the boss's authority and to rebel against the boss's decisions. Sometimes a person would escalate a conflict beyond what is appropriate. Seeing the boss almost as an institutional enemy, this type of staff would often, without being conscious of it, antagonize the boss just for the sake of confrontation. The manager's reactions to being constrained are usually strong and sometimes impulsive. He or she sees the boss as someone whose role is to hinder progress, an obstacle to be circumvented or at best tolerated.

Altering predispositions toward authority, especially at the extremes, is almost impossible without intensive psychotherapy (psychoanalytic theory and research suggest that such predispositions are deeply rooted in a person's personality and upbringing). However, an awareness of these extremes and the range between them can be very useful in understanding where your own predispositions fall and what the implications are for how you tend to behave in relation to your boss.

No doubt, some subordinates would resent that on top of all their other duties, they also need to take time and energy to manage their relationships with their bosses. Such managers fail to realize the importance of this activity and how it can simplify their jobs by eliminating potentially severe problems. Effective staff and or managers recognize that this part of their work is legitimate. Seeing themselves as ultimately responsible for what they achieve in an organization, they know that they need to establish and manage relationships with everyone on whom they are dependent—and that includes the boss.

Some bosses would argue the point until they win and they would not hesitate to use either raw power or a raised their voice in the absence of intellectual advantage. What is the root of this need to be right all the time? Do they really believe in the myth of their own genius? Do they really believe they are inerrant? It is as if they have seen all the facts and have concluded that nothing else is possible but their own point of view.

How does one avoid the position of being wrong in the business world? Why make a high-profile mistake when it could have been sorted out away from public glare? So, how do you walk your ego through this potential minefield? It is by bringing everyone in on the plan. They will recognize your visions even if it is short of necessary details. The details are the things that the manager delegates to others; therefore, there should be no ego conflict in his knowledge gap.

The boss invariably knows about your hard work and commitment to the job. Sometimes, however, he forgets to acknowledge your efforts. It is a fact that not every boss recognizes the need to motivate his employees. It is also important to remember that, if he does not praise a smart, hard-working employee like you, he has probably not praised anyone else. If you notice that a co-worker whom you think is a non-performer is often praised by the boss, do not give in to a knee-jerk reaction of thinking that you need to find a new boss. Instead, check and find out whether you can learn by observing what your praiseworthy co-worker does. You might be surprised.

This is often an issue between two teams or between departments, and you may feel that the boss favours a particular person or one entire department over another. In fact, it is virtually impossible to be a perfectly fair boss. In many cases, a department has to make sacrifices in the overall interest of the organization. A clever boss, however, should know when to make it up to all his subordinates. If you feel your department is constantly sacrificing or giving too much, this should not provide an excuse to reduce your loyalty or productivity. Different bosses have different levels of sensitivity about certain things. Some bosses may only focus on big issues such as cheating on expense claims; another may be sensitive to employees' punctuality, while yet another may insist on employees supporting each of his ideas. While we all would prefer tolerance, not every boss is capable of this. After all, they are only human and they do face a lot of pressure. Also, just like the rest of us, they have bad moods. When this happens, employees should try to be more understanding. Offer support when you can, you could sow a seed of tolerance in your boss.

If you do not repose confidence in yourself, nobody will. Staff must believe in themselves and their ability and resolve not to be treated like a pawn on a chess-board. On the bosses' part, they do not have to be ruthless to run an establishment. As a boss, you have to win your staff's love and trust by relating well with them despite their deficiencies. Frequent nagging may compel staff to feed the boss with lies in order to please them. If the boss is a complaining type, whenever he is not around, the staffs are likely to be very happy and wish that his vacation lasted longer. It is a sad situation when they have their happiest weeks or month because the boss is absent. Employees seldom work well with close monitoring; they require some space to display their best qualities such as initiative, dedication and loyalty.

In summary, there must be an open relationship between the boss and the members of staff. Inter-personal communication must be emphasized. The workplace, where workers typically spend at least a third of their day, should feel like home, Workers should derive pleasure from the work they do, just like many professional footballers have confessed about their vocation. The boss should be their role model. The Boss in this case Manager or Director has nothing to gain if the relationship between the staff and him is defined respectively by fear and oppression. A kind and considerate person is at peace with himself and his staff; he is also admired by the customers. Indeed, being a kind boss is a virtue.

Chapter Three

ORGANIZATION'S ROLE IN SELECTING WHO MANAGES WHO

Team work divides the task and multiplies the success. In every organization, there should be division of labour. Duties and responsibilities are usually designated to the head of each unit. This helps the organization to run smoothly in a competitive market. A team leader should be chosen based on experience. He must be goal oriented and possess the ability to co-ordinate others in the team, as well as welcome the ideas, advice and opinion of other members. Team work or team spirit should be priority. Every little thing counts and so everybody should be given an opportunity to contribute to the success of the task or project. The methodology of delivery should be well rehearsed and the necessary mechanism should be available to get the job done or the deal closed, despite some possible short-comings and challenges. One has to be fearless to survive in a competitive market.

Combined effort for collective result

Every organization needs growth and development. The boss should help the workers to grow and overcome the challenges which they might be facing at the work place. His word of advice could help them to close a deal that swells the company's account. The team leader must be disciplined and be in charge since success or recrimination is directed at him. Everybody in the unit must be on the same page and work towards its collective success. The team leader should ensure that no team member pulls back. He should control rather than abuse his veto power. Fault should be corrected politely and those who are not contributing enough should be called to order. As a team leader, not everyone would like your approach. Therefore, the leader should encourage members to contribute ideas. Everybody should be carried along in accordance with the adage that 'two good heads are better than one'. Information hoarding, self-centredness, negligence and witch-hunting leave negative consequences in their wake. A team leader should control his or her ego and constantly evaluate him or herself. Most importantly, he should choose the right words to communicate with his colleagues because everybody in the organization is significant. Someone's responsibility should be everybody responsibility. There should be an understanding in every unit. Respect is reciprocal and the team leader has to earn it. There should be free flow of communication made possible by the leader.

A project team leader must lead by example—which requires great sacrifice. Challenges must be embraced as an opportunity to learn something new. When a company is running at a loss, the organization role of selecting who manages who has failed. When the establishment is getting results, and accounts for the year end, the principal activities of the company in term of sales and technical support services, the turnover, the net profit for the year, taxation, profit after taxation, then the organization has put the right mechanism in place for the smooth operation of the company. The shareholders, directors, managers and staff have cause to be happy at the returns on their investment. The bottom line for any profit-oriented establishment is, of course, to make profit. Action is the statement of our commitment and it takes courage to take action.

> *"Go confidently in the direction of your dreams. Live the life you have imagined"*—*Henry David Thoreau.*

Chapter Four

PRIDE AS AN IMPEDIMENT TO INTER-PERSONAL WORKPLACE RELATIONSHIP

"In organizations, real power and energy are generated through relationships. The patterns of relationships and the capacities to form them are more important than tasks, functions, roles and positions."—Margaret Wheatly

Article I (9) of the United Nations Universal Declaration of Human Rights (UDHR) states: "All human beings are born free and equal in dignity and rights. They are endowed with reason and conscience and should act towards one brotherhood." On the basis of this premise, it is important for the boss to determine from the very beginning to carry his employees along in order to ensure effectiveness of the organization. Eschewing arrogance, he must realize that it is destiny and circumstances that have brought him and the employees together. They are not slaves but rather human beings with dignity who are sharing the vision of the boss and contributing toward the success of the organization. Instead of displaying a condescending attitude toward the workers, the boss should have a listening ear and be a true leader.

Employee creativity is honed on the platform of shared vision with the boss; the employee feels special and strives to do the impossible. In the first place, he was hired because the boss could not do all the work alone. Therefore, building the capacity of employees through seminars, workshops and other training programmes should be seen not as a waste of time and resources but as a means of enhancing productivity. The boss must see the workers as people who believe in his dream and vision towards the success of the business. Employers must bear in mind that employees will not work for them forever. *Opportunities may present for employees to move on to greener pastures and employers must be emotionally prepared when the time arrives.*

Close monitoring and undue pressure on the worker may result in a fall in productivity as employees become fidgety and demoralized. Rather than emphasize the negative, the boss should consciously identify, commend and encourage the strengths of the employees. In order to achieve and sustain a good level of productivity, workers must be encouraged to believe in themselves, the boss and the organization. On the other hand, arrogance on the part of the boss breeds negligence and inefficiency and hinders the flow of communication.

Every company wants its brand to be a household name. In order to achieve and sustain productivity, everybody must feel important towards the success of the company. A company is like a large ship; despite the large size, the ultimate authority in the movement and direction of the ship is the captain, and a small hole is capable of sinking it. However, the relationship between the boss and the employees is not a master-slave relationship. Both parties have been brought together by destiny or happenstance. At the appropriate time, the employees may take up other jobs, set up their own businesses, and so move on with their own lives.

Every profession has its ethics and methodology of delivery. Workers learn fast when given the necessary tools. A boss should encourage those who are performing well and support those who are yet to meet up with their targets. Pride can make a boss lose his best hands to a rival company with lucrative offers. They will not hesitate to resign and leave the job in a rude manner. A boss should show kind gestures to his workers for their contributions towards the growth and development of the company. The boss should have it at the back of his or her mind that inevitably they are learning and one day whey might start up their own businesses or get a better offer. How many bosses can give their workers blessing to start up their own businesses? You employed them and gave them job descriptions and over time, they become experts in the business and even explore more new grounds based on the opportunities you have made possible for them. It is natural for workers to be ambitious. However, the boss must remember that while the employee remains in the company and is doing extremely well, the credit goes to the boss. We are inter-independent, we are learning from one another. No man can be an island to himself and a tree cannot make a forest. Engaging a worker into a business is usually premised on his comparative advantage of skills. What he can do that others cannot do as well is what he will be paid for. It is wrong for a boss to humiliate his staff and conversely it is inappropriate for staff to thumb their noses at their boss. Honour should be accorded to whom it is due. The employee must realize that he cannot afford to show disrespect to someone who controls his pay cheque, pay raise, and promotion. There should be a mutual understanding between the two parties. The boss has an obligation to show kindness to people working under him since nobody knows tomorrow.

Often, pride would make a learned man not to ask for help. A professor once embarked on a journey. However, although he was not very familiar with airport processes, he was reluctant to seek guidance from fellow passengers and airport employees about what to do next. To his chagrin, when he finally sought help, his plane had departed five minutes earlier. It is wise to ask for help when the need arises. The professor realized this fact too late because of his pride.

A boss should be proud of his staff. When they are appreciated they tend to do more. Smiles should be put on their faces with extra cash. Training and workshops will help them to learn and re-learn and become useful to the organization and to themselves. Apart from pride, another sentiment that could adversely impact a business, from the point of view of the boss, is anger. The boss should speak in such a way that others love to listen to him, and listen in such a way that others love to speak to him.

> *"Good plans shape good decisions. That's why good planning helps to make elusive dreams come true."* Lester R. Bittel.

After considerable investment in time and money recruiting and training employees, it must now be determined how to make sure those valuable employees are productive, and get them to remain loyal to the firm. Retention of employees is essential to maintain client relationships and keep recruiting and training costs in line. Losing an experienced employee almost always results in significant costs to the firm. Employee satisfaction and retention are founded on strong leadership and sound management practices. If these arts could be mastered, the employees and clients would be happy and loyal, resulting in growth, profits and personal gratification. Let us now discuss key factors in motivating and retaining good people.

Operating Systems

The foundation of an efficient and effective workplace is the structure, discipline and consistency provided by well-conceived systematic operating methods. World-class companies all have well defined operating methods. A policies and procedures (P&P) manual is critical to ensure that employees understand what is expected of them and know how they should handle the myriad of duties and responsibilities in the day-to-day operation of the office. The P&P manual spells out how you would like things done in your office and your expectations for the behaviour of your employees. As your operation grows larger, the system becomes more important because your ability to oversee and communicate directly and frequently with each employee becomes more difficult. Written operating systems are absolutely essential when you expand to more than one office location. Creating an Intranet is also a good idea for large operations.

Training

In addition to training in policies and procedures, customer service and marketing should be covered at length. Special emphasis should be placed on corporate culture. New employees need more training than priors, but all employees should receive training each year. New employees should also have several days of on-the-job training with the office manager or experienced employees before beginning their position; and they should not be left on their own in the office until they are experienced enough to feel confident. Many of the frustrations employees feel on the job—as well as most errors and client problems—are due to inadequate training. Comprehensive training will make life as a manager much easier, and your employees and clients will be happier.

Tools to do the Job

Employee costs constitute the greatest expense in any service business. Not giving your employees adequate tools to do the job is penny wise and pound foolish. Computers need not be state-of-the-art, but they do need to be fast and reliable enough to minimize down time and reduce employee and client frustration. If your office is not operating with a Local Area Network (LAN), you should set one up without delay. A LAN manages printer sharing and centralizes client files for easy computer cross-checking, e-filing., and report writing. Copiers should be reliable and fast, with automatic feed, and ample supplies always on hand. A fax is no longer a costly luxury for most offices, but a necessity. Internet access is almost as important as the phone for effective communication and is becoming more essential for research. Don't forget to provide the little things, like reliable staplers, staple removers, scissors, pens, post-its, business card holders, etc. An appointment book, a Rolodex (or software address book), and reference books and resources should also be provided. Comfortable, functional office furniture and adequate shelving and storage are also essential. Also remember aids for employees with special needs, such as under-desk computer drawers and keyboard and mouse cushions. Use checklists of office furnishings, equipment and supplies used to take inventory and request missing or shortage items. Attention to detail and providing adequate tools to do the job will eliminate a key source of employee frustration and increase employee productivity and satisfaction.

Office Atmosphere

How your employees feel about their jobs is greatly influenced by your office atmosphere. Extravagance is not necessary, but the office should be attractively decorated and a pleasant place to work in. Little things like a fresh coat of paint and a wallpaper border make a big difference. A stereo (with ceiling speakers) tuned to a soft neutral music enhances the office atmosphere and creates an illusion of privacy. Don't neglect the back room and the rest room. We pay as much attention to decorating and appointing our rest rooms as we do our client reception areas. Provide a microwave and refrigerator for the back room of every office and, space permitting, a table and chairs where associates can eat. The impression you make on your employees is just as important as the image you project to your clients. Keeping the office clean and uncluttered requires the cooperation of all employees, and you should insist that every employee pitches in to help. However, you should regularly hire contractors for heavy cleaning (e.g., carpet, windows and restroom). Your employees' attitudes are affected by their physical work environment; make sure it is positive!

Support

Your employees will appreciate having adequate support. They need someone readily available to help when they have questions or encounter problems. Support can be provided on-site by an office manager or veteran employee or by telephone or e-mail when on-site help is not available. Having adequate help to properly serve all clients in the office is also essential for employee morale. The important point is that your people should not feel like they are out there on their own with no one to turn to when they need help. If they feel this way, they might as well go into business on their own.

Corporate Culture

World-class companies always have in common world-class cultures. Leaders of such businesses recognize that their companies exist to satisfy a social need. Profits are not the goal, but are a by-product of meeting the needs of customers and employees. Businesses also have a responsibility to give back to the communities in which they operate. Most employees also have a need to make meaningful contributions to society through their work. They also like to take pride in their work and deliver quality products and services. And they need to continue to learn and grow professionally. A good corporate culture enables employees to combine their strengths to meet these mutual needs as part of a dynamic team.

A company's culture starts with its mission and values, which should be well thought-out and articulated in writing. A mission statement and set of guiding principles are typically developed by the company's owner or CEO to reflect his or her business philosophy. Input should also be solicited from key employees. When hiring new employees, it is essential to confirm their understanding of, and agreement with, the company philosophy. The values must not be observed merely through lip service, but should be internalized and practised daily by all employees. The owner or CEO must set the standard for the employees.

Compensation

A performance-based compensation plan should be designed to encourage employees to behave in ways that will result in the attainment of company goals, while also meeting employees' personal objectives. Company goals usually include growth, profitability, quality service, efficiency, effectiveness, image and reputation. To attract desirable employees, base pay and earnings potential should be competitive within the industry (equal to or better than the main competitors for employees). The pay plan must be objective and fair to all employees. Rewards should be commensurate with contributions. Establishing a sound compensation plan is one of the most important projects the boss will undertake. Once the plan is established, it is difficult to make radical changes. A fair and just compensation plan is an essential element in the company's ability to compete effectively.

Benefits

Providing whatever reasonable benefits can put the company in a better competitive position to attract and retain seasonal employees. A profit-sharing plan could be adopted for all employees to enable them to share in the profit pool in proportion to their annual earnings relative to total earnings of all employees. The profit pool could be some percentage (e.g. 10-20% as determined by management) of the increase in pre-tax profits over the previous year. Little perks, such as buying pizza for the staff of the office on the busiest days of the work week, help to make employees appreciate their jobs. Some creativity is required here.

Recognitions

Numerous studies and surveys have documented the fact that money is not always the primary motivator for most employees. Frequent recognition for good work is likely to engender more sterling performance. Praise must be sincere and should be distributed equitably, if merited. When possible, employees should be praised publicly at meetings or in employee newsletters. Be sure to give people credit and rewards for good ideas which they come up with that benefit the company. Reinforce the right behaviours. Avoid saying "Great but." Look for key measures to recognize employees, such as production, client retention rate, etc. Contests could be organized to recognize performing employees, such as the most referrals for another service offered by the company, or the most new clients brought in. Recognition certificates, plaques, prizes, tickets for movie rental or sports events, or gift certificates for merchandise or dinner could all come in handy as incentives to employees. Tangible gifts make a more lasting impression. Praising and appreciating high performers (the top 10-20%) will raise the bar for weaker people. The goal is to encourage behaviours that build the business and recognize people for practicing those behaviours as often as possible.

Communication

Lack of effective communication from management is usually the greatest cause of employee dissatisfaction and premature departure. The best managers listen to and communicate frequently with all employees; and they make it easy for employees to tell them about problems and concerns. Communication should include training, group and individual meetings and, most important, daily discussions between the boss and his employees. The larger the organization becomes, the more difficult it is to keep in touch with all employees, especially in a multiple-office situation. Yet, the manager must make the time to regularly talk with everyone. E-mail is a good communication vehicle, but the phone is more personal; and neither can replace face-to-face meetings. Publishing employee newsletters is a good way for larger organizations to enhance communication. An Intranet can also be an effective internal communication vehicle. Communication must be kept simple, with adequate information and examples for clarity. Trust should be demonstrated continually and the people made to feel included by sharing with them financial and other company inside information. Management can make much better decisions by getting input from front-line employees. If workers know that their voices are heard and they feel like they are part of the decision-making process, they will be much happier, loyal and more likely to support new ideas and programs.

Empowerment

Employees should be co-opted into the decision-making process and given the authority to act in the best interest of the company. Training should be provided for resolving client problems, and staff involved should be trusted to make the right decisions. Employees should be given some time to think and plan by building in some slack through adequate staffing and by providing clerical support. Employee mistakes should not be unduly criticized; instead honest mistakes should be celebrated. It should be recognized that making decisions naturally results in making mistakes because no one is perfect. If you over-criticize or ridicule honest mistakes, your people will stop making decisions. Failure is also not a bad thing per se, because it is a normal part of the road to success. Nothing is more gratifying than to see one's workers develop the skills and confidence to act independently and to make sound decisions that are in the best interest of the company and its clients.

Leadership

Here are ten basic keys to be a more effective leader:

(1) Integrity: Always tell the truth and always keep your promise, even if it hurts to do so.
(2) Trust: You must first demonstrate your trust in people by making yourself vulnerable before you can expect them to place their trust in you.
(3) Respect: If you really don't care about your people they will sense your lack of concern and will not have respect for you.

(4) Fairness: Treat all employees fairly and equally (including family members) regardless of your personal feelings.

(5) Vision: To be a true leader, you must have an unfaltering vision, be able to communicate it to your people, and get them to understand and share in your excitement for the vision.

(6) Optimism: You must always be positive and confident that the company will succeed; but you should also be realistic.

(7) Decisiveness: A leader must make decisions and stick with them as long as they make sense. Consensus is not always better than an individual decision, particularly in a crisis situation. Remember, the buck stops with you! Trust your intuition. Intuition draws upon your experience, stored knowledge and information you may not even realize you have in your head.

(8) Example: You must practice what you preach or you will have little credibility.

(9) Teamwork: Insist on mutual respect, courtesy and cooperation among your people. This fundamental attitude was crucial in shaping many great nations and is also essential to build your company.

(10) Authority: Remember that authority is not vested in your position as the boss. Authority resides with the people who report to you and they have the power to grant it to you or not.

Having Fun

People like to work in an environment that is enjoyable; they can get burned out if the work environment is totally serious and strictly business.

Great companies have come up with creative ways for employees to have fun. If the boss is not naturally good at getting people to have fun, a key employee should be designated to assume this role.

In summary, motivating and keeping employees requires effective management practices and strong leadership skills. Workers need an operating system, and adequate training is essential. They need the proper tools and support to do the job. A performance-based compensation plan should be designed very carefully to ensure that employees are encouraged to help build the business and are rewarded for their contributions, and provide as many extra benefits as possible. A positive corporate culture and a pleasant work environment are more important than money to most good employees. Recognition and communication are among the key responsibilities of a manager. Screening new employment prospects to ensure that they fit in and buy into the company's culture will prevent future problems. Employment agreements are imperative and should be reviewed by and explained to new hires. Employees should be trusted, included and empowered to make decisions and act autonomously. They also need to be part of a harmonious team working for the mutual benefit of the clients, the company and themselves. Ultimately, the management and leadership skills and efforts of the boss will determine his success in providing an atmosphere where employees are motivated to be effective and remain loyal to the company.

Chapter Five

PROFITABILITY DEPENDS ON HARMONIOUS BOSS-SUBORDINATE RELATIONSHIP

Studies suggest that effective managers take time and effort to manage not only relationships with their subordinates but also those with their bosses. These studies show as well that this aspect of management, essential though it is to survival and advancement, is sometimes ignored by otherwise talented and aggressive managers. Indeed, some managers who actively and effectively supervise subordinates, products, markets, and technologies, nevertheless assume an almost passively reactive stance vis-a-vis their bosses. Such a stance practically always hurts these managers and their companies.

If you doubt the importance of managing your relationship with your boss or how difficult it is to do so effectively, consider for a moment this sad but true story:

John Smith was an acknowledged manufacturing genius in his industry and, by any profitability standard, a very effective executive. His strengths propelled him into the position of president of manufacturing for the second-largest and most profitable company in its industry. Smith was not, however, a good manager of people. He knew this, as did others in his company and his industry. Recognizing this weakness, the president made sure that those who reported to Smith were good at working with people and could compensate for his limitations. The arrangement worked well. Two years later, Alex Philip was promoted into a position reporting to Smith. In keeping with the previous pattern, the president selected Philip because he had an excellent track record and a reputation for being good with people. In making that selection, however, the president neglected to notice that, in his rapid rise through the organization, Philip himself had never reported to anyone who was poor at managing subordinates. Philip had always had good-to-excellent bosses. He had never been forced to manage a relationship with a difficult boss. In retrospect, Philip admits he had never thought that managing his boss was a part of his job.

Fourteen months after he started working for Smith, Philip was fired. During that same quarter, the company reported a net loss for the first time in seven years. Many of those who were close to these events; say that they don't really understand what happened. This much is known, however: while the company was bringing out a major new product—a process that required its sales, engineering, and manufacturing groups to coordinate their decisions very carefully—a whole series of misunderstandings and bad feelings developed between Smith and Philip.

For example, Philip claims Smith was aware of and had accepted Philip's decision to use a new type of machinery to make the new product; Smith swears he did not. Furthermore, Smith claims he made it clear to Philip that introduction of the product was too important to the company in the short run to take any major risks.

As a result of such misunderstandings, planning went awry: a new manufacturing plant was built that could not produce the new product designed by engineering, in the volume desired by sales, at a cost agreed on by the executive committee. Smith blamed Philip for the mistake. Philip blamed Smith.

Of course, one could argue that the problem here was caused by Smith's inability to manage his subordinates. But one can make just as strong a case that the problem was related to Philip's inability to manage his boss. Remember, Smith was not having difficulty with any other subordinates. Moreover, given the personal price paid by Philip (being fired and having his reputation within the industry severely tarnished), there was little consolation in saying the problem was that Smith was poor at managing subordinates. Everyone already knew that.

We believe that the situation could have turned out differently had Philip been more adept at understanding Smith and at managing his relationship with him. In this case, an inability to manage upward was unusually costly. The company lost $2 to $5 million, and Philip's career was, at least temporarily, disrupted. Many less costly cases like this probably occur regularly in all major corporations, and the cumulative effect can be very destructive. People often dismiss stories like this one as being merely cases of personality conflict. Because two people can on occasion be psychologically or temperamentally incapable of working together, this can be an apt description. But more often, we have found, a personality conflict is only a part of the problem—sometimes a very small part.

Philip did not just have a different personality from Smith; he also made or had unrealistic assumptions and expectations about the very nature of boss-subordinate relationships. Specifically, he did not recognize that his relationship to Smith involved *mutual dependence between two fallible human beings*. Failing to recognize this, a manager typically either avoids trying to manage his or her relationship with a boss or manages it ineffectively.

Some people behave as if their bosses were not very dependent on them. They fail to see how much the boss needs their help and cooperation to do his or her job effectively. These people refuse to acknowledge that the boss can be severely hurt by their actions and needs cooperation, dependability, and honesty from them.

Some see themselves as not very dependent on their bosses. They gloss over how much help and information they need from the boss in order to perform their own jobs well. This superficial view is particularly damaging when a manager's job and decisions affect other parts of the organization, as in Philip's situation. A manager's immediate boss can play a critical role in linking the manager to the rest of the organization, in making sure the manager's priorities are consistent with organizational needs, and in securing the resources the manager needs to perform well. Yet some managers need to see themselves as practically self-sufficient, as not needing the critical information and resources a boss can supply.

Many managers, like Philip, assume that the boss will magically know what information or help their subordinates need and provide it to them. Certainly, some bosses do an excellent job of caring for their subordinates in this way, but for a manager to expect that from all bosses is dangerously unrealistic. A more reasonable expectation for managers to have is that modest help will be forthcoming. Most really effective managers accept this fact and assume primary responsibility for their own careers and development. They make a point of seeking the information and help they need to do a job instead of waiting for their bosses to provide it.

Chapter Six

HOW IS CO-OPERATION POSSIBLE DESPITE THE BOSS' DEFICIENCIES?

The boss is the boss. He or she may own the business. The employee is hired for a job description. He has to make the boss feel in charge or he might appear over—ambitious. The employee was chosen because he fit a job description not the boss position. Some bosses with deficiencies may prove difficult in the sense that the employee's moves might be perceived as a threat to them. The employee might be called to order and told that there are policies and procedures for doing things in the company. If he does not adjust, he might be sacked. One needs wisdom to relate with bosses who are incapable of apologizing when they are wrong. The trend these days seems to be that the boss rarely apologizes to his staff. A wise staff would play along. First and foremost, in a staff meeting for example, the subordinate acknowledges the boss' position on a matter and builds his contribution around the boss' ideas. In most cases, the boss should be allowed to take the credit for the job, bearing in mind that the employee's own day in the limelight will come.

Making the boss feel redundant could spark conflict in an organization. Moreover, some bosses know that they have some shortcomings. So, they get the best hands and learn from them. The boss is bound to be jealous and resentful of a cocky and over-zealous subordinate. If the boss is embarking on a project that could cost the company a fortune, the employee is duty-bound to point out the danger, albeit with due respect. If the situation of properly handled, the boss is likely to agree with the subordinate who standing would subsequently be enhanced in the eyes of the boss.

According to Baltasar Gracion, "the path to greatness is along with others." A sensitive worker builds on the ideas of his boss. The employee cannot discard the boss' suggestions off hand. If you are invited to a meal, you do not impede or prevent your host from partaking in the repast. It is good to know the pros and cons of a business before delving into it. A boss that has deficiencies doesn't compete with the expert working for him or her. The boss' initial knowledge about the business, fused with input from the workers will work tremendous good for cohesion in the company. Seminars, conferences and workshops are good for both the boss and his subordinate despite the financial implications. After all, as the saying goes, "If knowledge is expensive; one should try ignorance."

All that the employee needs to do is play along with the boss in order to get the job done. The boss must be allowed to feel in charge so as to prevent ill-feelings. Let the boss dominate the speech at the staff meeting, and the staffs contribute only if called upon to do so. Although a co-worker may be disagreeable, the employee must avoid arguments because workers who constantly argue may be fired. In a perfect world, the best candidates quickly climb organizational ladders. But it's not a perfect world and unqualified candidates end up with great jobs for all the wrong reasons. Heading the list are cronyism (never underestimate the power of good old boys networks), seniority and nepotism (daddy owns the company).

Consider how new employees feel about reporting to an incompetent manager. Once settled into the new job, the signs of incompetence are blatantly obvious. They include:

Inability to make decisions: An incompetent boss often waffles over decisions that should be made instantly. Try not to make them feel bad but offer your support.

Tendency to make bad choices: Ineffectual bosses are likely to make poorly planned, miscalculated decisions.

Ability to keep the job despite failings: It is shocking how many inept bosses hold on to their jobs despite their failings. Typically, they rely on subordinates to get them through hard times. They could sometimes be rude to you, that is the sign of them trying to hang on, support them with your skills and you will shine.

Take advantage of the situation
The situation may look far worse than it actually is. So, one should not be quick to jump ship. Learning to adjust could be a career-enhancing experience. Incredible as it may seem, the boss' ineptitude could be a blessing.

Consider that it is an opportunity to stand out by becoming an asset to your boss. The more one does and accomplishes, the better it looks on one's resume. It also scores points with management, but do your job with utmost respect, learn to carry your boss along and you will be a star. Never make your boss lose control.

Career opportunity

Here are four strategies that could turn unfortunate circumstances into an advantage:

1. **Cover in a crisis**. If the boss is away on a business trip or vacation and an issue requiring instant decision-making arises, the subordinate has two choices: either turn the problem over to a senior manager or make the decision himself. Calling in senior managers makes the boss look bad. It is better to take the initiative and make the decision himself. Remember that heroes are born in crisis situations.

2. **Compensate for deficiencies.** It is to the subordinate's advantage to discover the boss' weak points and help him in those areas. It must not be forgotten that despite his shortcomings, he is still the boss, and deserves all the courtesies his position deserves. By the same token, the employee should observe his boss closely in order to spot his deficiencies. He may be unable to make fast decisions in emergency situations, for example. He may lack the confidence or knowledge to analyse a situation and propose a course of action. Or he may be stymied or immobilized by complex problems. These are ideal situations for the subordinate to step in and render an opinion or suggestion. But it must be done strategically and in such a way as not to steal the boss' thunder. If the ideas are presented respectfully, he is likely to quickly see that the proffered solutions make sense. The subordinate could subsequently become, as it were, the power behind the throne.

3. **The boss' shortcomings, the subordinate's opportunity**. In fact, it could lead to a rapid promotion or a transfer to another department. Rather than just do his job well, the staff should look for opportunities to take on new projects. The tougher the task, the better. It could be worthwhile in the long run to frequently put in extra hours or even an occasional weekend.

4. **Great work attracts the attention of senior management.** Management is impressed by workers who are willing to go beyond their job description and solve problems which no one else can, or bothers with. The efforts of the enterprising staff will be noticed, because good work travels fast on the organizational grapevine. Management is always looking for superstars. Determining your skill deficiencies and repairing them can help avoid job loss. Pay careful attention during performance reviews

What to Do If the Boss Is Incompetent

Incompetent bosses abound; thousands of unqualified bosses somehow manage to hold on to their jobs. There are even inept CEOs who could not run a broom closet, let alone multimillion-dollar corporations. However, the employee must be very wary about what he says about the boss and to whom, and keep his opinion to himself. It is quite easy to complain and vent frustrations about the less-than-qualified boss to co-workers. Without realizing it, one could be talking to the boss' good friend or someone who wants to score points with him.

Chapter Seven

LEADERSHIP AND FRIENDSHIP

According to Warren Bennis, "a new leader has to be able to change an organization that is dreamless, soulless and visionless . . . someone's got to make a wake-up call". Napoleon Bonaparte also describes a leader as "a dealer in hope". Almost everyone can stand adversity, but if you wish to test a man's character, give him power. Great power comes with great responsibility and, as the saying goes, power corrupts and absolute power corrupts absolutely. Visionary leaders motivate their followers and regard their position as a privilege to be deployed in the interest of a worthy cause rather than an instrument for oppression and self-aggrandizement. As Max Depree puts it, "leaders don't inflict pain; they bear pain".

If you aim at pleasing everybody you will end up displeasing yourself. A leader must be available when the need arises. He must be alert and always be a problem-solver. He must represent his colleagues and respect their suggestions and comments. The true test of a leader is to lead, and lead aright and be prepared to accept vicarious responsibility when things go wrong rather than attempt to cover up and give excuses.

There will be division of vision when your friends are not in support of you.

The leader must be on the same page with his colleagues. He does not allow the leadership position to get into his head. The leader must avoid unnecessary conflict by refraining from imposing his will on his colleagues. Rather he should seek their opinion on vital issues.

In the real world of work, emotions and relationships cannot be governed by policy. Workplace relationships can be extremely tricky, just as

Managers are not robots—they have feelings and emotions. Perhaps it would be helpful to refer to the definition of "friend". According to Merriam-Webster Dictionary, a friend is "one attached to another through affection or esteem; one that is not hostile, a favoured companion." No matter how close a manager may feel to an employee, it should never be confused with real "friendship". One might be a "friendly" boss, and the relationship may even share some of the characteristics of true friendship. One might even refer to it "a friend with boundaries". However, the role of a manager transcends friendship and creates a boundary and potential scenarios that would never exist between true friends.

If a manager allows himself to become emotionally attached to one employee—for whatever reason—those emotions are likely to consciously or unconsciously influence decisions around raises, layoffs, assignments, and promotions. Such favouritism is also bound to endanger the workplace camaraderie. An example of this, albeit in a different context, could be found in the biblical account of Joseph whose father Jacob openly demonstrated his preference for him over his eleven brothers, and made for him the famed "coat of many colours". When the resultant jealousy brimmed over, the brothers almost murdered Joseph but changed their minds at the last minute and sold him into slavery instead.

Part of the responsibilities of a manager is to supervise the employees, give constructive feedback, and sometimes discipline them, even fire them. All employees may have reason to complain about their bosses every now and then, and not even the best managers are immune to this. However, if the manager sees his employees as friends, he is more likely to take it personally.

Managers are supposed to set examples and be role models. Therefore, as a "manager-friend", he is going to be a boring uptight, friend, or an unprofessional, immature manager. Is it right for a manager to socialize with his employees? Or go out for a drink? Certainly, as long as he makes it a habit to stick to one drink and be the first to leave (to give them time to complain about him), or at least not the *last* to leave. Some employees may actually find the manager's attempts to be friends as personally intrusive, or inappropriate. They might even find his "advances" to be creating a hostile work environment, and again, exposing himself and the company.

According to Thomas Rosicky, "sometimes success is closer than you think." But the leader must appreciate the inherent challenges of his position, and make the necessary sacrifice. There should be healthy relationship between the leader and the followers. He must not take the support of the followers in all circumstances for granted. Often, followers lend the support to the leader based on their personal perception of how the leader's attitude and actions impact on their own welfare. A leader who understands this would take measures to avoid misunderstanding, rage and conspiracy among the followers. There will be misaligned vision if your friends do not agree with your views. In order not to lose his friends, a leader must carry them along on the business plan.

Chapter Eight

THE UNTOLD DIFFERENCES BETWEEN LEADERSHIP AND MANAGEMENT

LEADERSHIP

"The quality of leadership, more than any other single factor, determines the success or failure of an organization." Fred Fiedler.

Leadership is a tough quality to define. Our definition of leadership needs to change for a knowledge-driven world that is no longer rigidly hierarchical, stable or static but one that is fluid, fast-changing and less formally structured.

Leadership has always been based on power. For the conventional view, this means the power of personality to dominate a group. Leadership has been described as the "process of social influence in which one person can enlist the aid and support of others in the accomplishment of a common task" (Chemers M. 1997) other in-depth definitions of leadership have also emerged. Leadership is "organizing a group of people to achieve a common goal". The leader may or may not have any formal authority. Students of leadership have produced theories involving traits (Locke et al. 1991), situational interaction, function, behaviour, power, vision and values (Richards & Engle, 1986, p.206), charisma, and intelligence, among others. **Leadership is an interactive conversation that pulls people toward becoming comfortable with the language of personal responsibility and commitment.** Leadership can be defined as one's ability to get others to willingly follow. Every organization needs leaders at every level.

A leader is a person who influences a group of people towards a specific result. It is not dependent on title or formal authority. Ogbonnia (2007) defines an effective leader "as an individual with the capacity to consistently succeed in a given condition and be viewed as meeting the expectations of an organisation or society." Leaders are recognized by their capacity for caring for others, clear communication, and a commitment to persist (Hoyle, John R.1995).

Leaders emerge from within the structure of the informal organization. Their personal qualities, the demands of the situation, or a combination of these and other factors attract followers who accept their leadership within one or several overlay structures. Instead of the authority of position held by an appointed head or chief, the emergent leader wields influence or power. Influence is the ability of a person to gain co-operation from others by means of persuasion or control over rewards. Power is a stronger form of influence because it reflects a person's ability to enforce action through the control of a means of punishment.

In Galton's *Hereditary Genius* (1869), he examined leadership qualities in the families of powerful men. After showing that the numbers of eminent relatives dropped off when moving from first degree to second degree relatives, Galton concluded that leadership was inherited. In other words, leaders were born, not developed. Both of these notable works lent great initial support for the notion that leadership is rooted in characteristics of the leader. Equipped with new methods, leadership researchers revealed the following:

- Individuals can and do emerge as leaders across a variety of situations and tasks.
- Significant relationships exist between leadership and such individual

Traits as:

- intelligence
- adjustment
- extraversion
- conscientiousness
- openness to experience
- general self-efficacy

Leadership Styles

Leadership style refers to a leader's behaviour. It is the result of the philosophy, personality, and experience of the leader. Rhetoric specialists have also developed models for understanding leadership (Robert Hariman, *Political Style*, Philippe-Joseph Salazar, L'Hyperpolitique. *Technologies politiques De La Domination*).

Different situations call for different leadership styles. In an emergency when there is little time to converge on an agreement and where a designated authority has significantly more experience or expertise than the rest of the team, an autocratic leadership style may be most effective; however, in a highly motivated and aligned team with a homogeneous level of expertise, a more democratic or laissez-faire style may be more effective. The style adopted should be the one that most effectively achieves the objectives of the group while balancing the interests of its individual members.

Autocratic or authoritarian style
Under the autocratic leadership style, all decision-making powers are centralized in the leader, as with dictators.

Leaders do not entertain any suggestions or initiatives from subordinates. The autocratic management has been successful as it provides strong motivation to the manager. It permits quick decision-making, as only one person decides for the whole group and keeps each decision to him or herself until he or she feels it needs to be shared with the rest of the group.

Participative or democratic style
The democratic leadership style favours decision-making by the group. Such a leader gives instructions after consulting the group.

They can win the cooperation of their group and can motivate them effectively and positively. The decisions of the democratic leader are not unilateral as with the autocrat because they arise from consultation with the group members and participation by them.

Laissez-faire or free rein style
A free-rein leader does not lead, but leaves the group entirely to itself. Such a leader allows maximum freedom to subordinates; they are given a free hand in deciding their own policies and methods.

Attributes of a Leader

While leadership is certainly difficult to define, there are attributes that we can associate with a good leader.

1. **Visionary**: A leader brings a vision to his group; it is a plan which others can follow. This vision brings the followers the emotion of hope and something they can strive to achieve. This should be clear with the leader standing up for what he believes

   "A leader is a dealer in hope"
   —Napoleon Bonaparte

2. **Reliable**: You don't want to follow someone that shows up late or does not do what they say they are going to do. In a leader, you want someone who is reliable, with a message that people can follow. If leaders are not consistent in their efforts and their actions, it causes followers to begin to doubt the dedication of the leader to the cause. A historian, Doris Kearns Goodwin, stated that during the Great Depression, a citizen once said something to the effect that "I don't have any money, don't have a job, and I don't have a reason to live, but I keep on going because I know hope is there."

   "Delegating work works,
   provided the one delegating works, too."
   —Robert Half

3. **Audacity**: It takes guts to be a leader; it is not for everyone. Some people satisfied with

tagging along for the ride. Not everyone can or should be a leader.

4. **Empowering People**: Inherently, people want to do a good job. They want to succeed and make others happy. A leader should encourage people to succeed. By empowering people, the leader is not necessarily doing the task for the followers but instead gives them the tools necessary to succeed.

5. **Positive**: Nobody wants to follow a person who is "doom and gloom." A leader does not need to be all about rainbows and sunshine, but there definitely should be a boost of positivity, especially when tackling a difficult project or when the "going gets tough."

> **"A pessimist sees the difficulty in every opportunity; an optimist sees the opportunity in every difficulty."**
> **—Winston Churchill**

6. **Motivating**: If the above-mentioned characteristics are absent, the follower will certainly not be motivated to follow the leader let alone do a great job. A leader needs a vision; otherwise the followers do not have a map and tend to get lost.

Leadership Myths

Leadership, although largely talked about, has been described as one of the least understood concepts across all cultures and civilizations. Over the years, many researchers have stressed the prevalence of this misunderstanding, stating that the existence of several flawed assumptions, or myths, concerning leadership often interferes with the individual's conception of what leadership is all about (Gardner, 1965; Bennis, 1975).

Leadership is innate

According to some, leadership is determined by distinctive dispositional characteristics present at birth (e.g., extraversion; intelligence; ingenuity). However, it is important to note that leadership also develops through hard work and careful observation. Thus, effective leadership can result from nature (i.e., innate talents) as well as nurture (i.e., acquired skills).

Leadership is possessing power over others

Although leadership is certainly a form of power, it is not demarcated by power *over* people; rather, it is a power *with* people that exists as a reciprocal relationship between a leader and his or her followers (Forsyth, 2009). Despite popular belief, the use of manipulation, coercion, and domination to influence others is not a requirement for leadership. In fact, individuals who seek group consent and strive to act in the best interest of others can also become effective leaders (e.g., class president; court judge).

Leaders are positively influential

The validity of the assertion that groups flourish when guided by effective leaders can be illustrated using several examples. For instance, according to Baumeister et al. (1988), the bystander effect (failure to respond or offer assistance) that tends to develop within groups faced with an emergency is significantly reduced in groups guided by a leader. (Baumeister, R. F., Senders, P. S., Chesner, S. C., & Tice, D. M, 1988) Moreover, it has been documented that group performance, creativity, and efficiency all tend to climb in businesses with designated managers or CEOs. However, the difference leaders make is **not** always positive in nature. Leaders sometimes focus on fulfilling their own agendas at the expense of others, including his or her own followers. This assertion is tragically borne out by Pol Pot, the Cambodian despot who committed unspeakable atrocities including genocide against his people in the 1970s, and Josef Stalin, the Soviet dictator, who ruled his communist empire with an iron fist for all of three decades. Leaders who focus on personal gain by employing stringent and manipulative leadership style often make a difference, but usually do so through negative means.

Leaders entirely control group outcomes

In Western cultures, it is generally assumed that group leaders make *all* the difference when it comes to group influence and overall goal attainment. Although common, this romanticized view of leadership (i.e., the tendency to overestimate the degree of control leaders have over their groups and their groups' outcomes) ignores the existence of many other factors that influence group dynamics. (Meindl, J.R., Ehrlich, S.B., & Dukerich, J.M, 1985) For example, group cohesion, communication patterns among members, individual personality traits, group context, the nature or orientation of the work, as well as behavioural norms and established standards influence group functionality in varying capacities. For this reason, it is wrong to assume that all leaders are in complete control of their groups' achievements.

All groups have a designated leader

Despite preconceived notions, not all groups need have a designated leader. Groups that are primarily composed of women, are limited in size, are free from stressful decision-making, or only exist for a short period of time (e.g., student work groups; pub quiz/trivia teams) often undergo a diffusion of responsibility, where leadership tasks and roles are shared amongst members (Schmid Mast, 2002; Berdahl & Anderson, 2007; Guastello, 2007).

Group members resist leaders

Although research has indicated that group members' dependence on group leaders can lead to reduced self-reliance and overall group strength, most people actually prefer to be led than to be without a leader (Berkowitz, 1953). This "need for a leader" becomes especially strong in troubled groups that are experiencing some sort of conflict. Group members tend to be more contented and productive when they have a leader to guide them. Although individuals filling leadership roles can be a direct source of resentment for followers, most people appreciate the contributions that leaders make to their groups and consequently welcome the guidance of a leader (Stewart & Manz, 1995).

Management

Over the years the philosophical terminology of "management" and "leadership" have, in the organizational context, been used both as synonyms and with clearly differentiated meanings. Debate is fairly common about whether the use of these terms should be restricted, and generally reflects an awareness of the distinction made by Burns (1978) between "transactional" leadership (characterized by e.g. emphasis on procedures, contingent reward, management by exception) and "transformational" leadership (characterized by e.g. charisma, personal relationships, creativity).(Burns, J. M., 1978)

According to **Harold Koontz**, "Management is the art of getting things done through and with people in formally organized groups." According to **Henri Fayol**, "To manage is to forecast and to plan, to organize, to command, to co-ordinate and to control." According to **Mary Parker Follet**, "Management is the art of getting things done through people."

Management is an individual or a group of individuals that accept responsibilities to run an organisation. They *plan, organise, direct* and *control* all the essential activities of the organisation. Management does not do the work themselves. They motivate others to do the work and co-ordinate (i.e. bring together) all the work for achieving the objectives of the organisation. Management brings together all **Six Ms** i.e. Men (and Women), Money, Machines, Materials, Methods and Markets. They use these resources for achieving the objectives of the organisation such as high sales, maximum profits, and business expansion.

Features of Management

The nature, main **characteristics** or features of management are:-

1. Continuous and never ending process
Management is a Process. It includes four main functions, viz., Planning, Organising, Directing and Controlling. The manager has to *plan* and *organise* all the activities. He must give proper *directions* to his subordinates. It is also his responsibility to *control* all the activities. The manager is obliged to perform these functions continuously. Therefore, management is a continuous and never ending process.

2. Getting things done through people

Managers do not do the work themselves; they rather get the work done through the workers. The workers should not be treated like slaves; they should not be tricked, threatened or forced to do the work. A favourable work environment should be created and maintained.

3. Result oriented science and art

Management is result oriented because it gives a lot of importance to "**Results**". Examples of Results include increase in market share, increase in profits, etc. Management always aims at getting the best results at all times.

4. Multidisciplinary in nature

Management has to get the work done through people, i.e. it has to manage people. This is a very difficult task because different people have different emotions, feelings, aspirations, etc. Similarly, the same person may have different emotions at different times. So, management is a very complex undertaking. It is multi-disciplinary, using knowledge from many different subjects such as Economics, Information Technology, Psychology, Sociology, etc.

5. A group and not an individual activity

Management is not an individual activity; it is rather a group activity. It uses group (employees) efforts to achieve group (owners) objectives. It tries to satisfy the needs and wants of a group (consumers). Nowadays, importance is given to the team (group) and not to individuals.

6. Follows established principles or rules

Management follows established principles, such as division of work, discipline, unity of command, etc. These principles help to prevent and solve the problems in the organisation.

7. Aided but not replaced by computers

Nowadays, all managers use computers. Computers help the managers to take accurate decisions. However, computers can only help management; they cannot replace management. This is because management takes the final responsibility.

8. Situational in nature

Management makes plans, policies and decisions according to the situation. It changes its style according to the situation. It uses different plans, policies, decisions and styles for different situations.

The manager first studies the full present situation, draws conclusions about the situation then he makes plans, decisions, etc. which are best for the present situation. This is called **Situational** Management.

9. Need not be an ownership

In small organisations, management and ownership are one and the same. However, in large organisations, management is separate from ownership. The managers are highly qualified professionals who are hired from outside. The owners are the shareholders of the company.

10. Both an art and science

Management is result-oriented. Therefore, it is an Art. Management conducts continuous research. Thus, it is also a Science.

11. Management is all pervasive

Management is necessary for running a business and also essential for running, educational, charitable and religious institutions. Management is imperative for all activities, and therefore, it is all pervasive.

12. Management is intangible

Management is intangible, i.e. it cannot be seen and touched, but it can be felt and recognized by its results. The success or failure of management can be judged only by its results. If there is good discipline, good productivity, good profits, etc., then the management is successful and vice-versa.

13. Use a professional approach in work

Managers use a professional approach for getting the work done from their subordinates. They delegate (i.e. give) authority to their subordinates. They ask their subordinates to give suggestions for improving their work. They also encourage subordinates to take the initiative. Initiative means to do the right thing at the right time without being guided or helped by the superior.

14. Management is dynamic in nature

Management is dynamic in nature. That is, management is creative and innovative. An organisation will survive and succeed only if it is dynamic. It must continuously bring in new and creative ideas, new products, new product features, new ads, new marketing techniques, etc.

Leadership and Management

What is leadership, and what is the difference between leadership and management? In a nutshell, the difference is:

- Leadership is setting a new direction or vision for a group that they follow, i.e. a leader is the spearhead for that new direction
- Management controls or directs people/ resources in a group according to principles or values that have already been established.

By saying that leadership means promoting new directions, such as new products and services, everyone can show leadership. This means that CEOs manage as much as lead. However, we need to upgrade management to make it a more positive concept. At present, management is cast in a negative light. Leadership = promoting new directions by example or advocating for a better way. It works through influence, not by making decisions for people. Management = getting things done in a way that makes best use of all resources. The difference between leadership and management can be illustrated by considering what happens when you have one without the other.

Leadership without management
. . . sets a direction or vision that others follow, without much consideration of how the new direction is going to be achieved. Other people then have to work hard in the trail that is left behind, picking up the pieces and making it work. For example, in *Lord of the Rings*, at the Council of Elrond, Frodo Baggins rescues the council from conflict by taking responsibility for the quest of

destroying the ring, but most of the management of the group comes from others.

Management without leadership

. . . controls resources to maintain the status quo or ensure that things happen according to already-established plans. For example, a referee manages a sports game, but does not usually provide "leadership" because there is no change, no new direction. The referee is controlling resources to ensure that the laws of the game are followed and the status quo is maintained.

Leadership combined with management

. . . does both; it both sets a new direction and manages the resources to achieve it. An example is a newly elected president or prime minister.

Some potential confusion

The absence of leadership should not be confused with the type of leadership that calls for 'no action' to be taken. For example, when Mahatma Gandhi went on hunger strike and called for protests to stop, during the negotiations for India's independence, he demonstrated great leadership, because taking no action was a new direction for the Indian people at that time.

Also, what is often referred to as "participative management" can be a very effective form of leadership. In this approach, a new direction may seem to emerge from the group rather than the leader. However, the leader has facilitated that new direction whilst also engendering ownership within the group i.e., it is an advanced form of leadership.

Sometimes, an individual may act as a figure head for change and be viewed as a leader even though he or she has not set any new direction. This can arise when a group sets a new direction of its own accord, and needs to express that new direction in the form of a symbolic leader. An example is Nelson Mandela whilst in prison:

- While Nelson Mandela remained imprisoned (thus limiting his ability to provide personal, direct leadership), he continued to grow in power and influence as the *symbolic* leader for the anti-apartheid movement.
- Following his release from prison, he demonstrated *actual* leadership by leading South Africa into a process of reconciliation rather than retribution.

Leadership and Management: Summary

Leadership is about setting a new direction for a group; management is about directing and controlling according to established principles. However, someone can be a symbolic leader if they emerge as the spearhead of a direction the group sets for itself.

Managing Your Leader

This term is used to mean the process of consciously working with your superior to obtain the best possible results for you, your boss, and the company. Studies suggest that effective managers take time and effort to manage not only relationships with their subordinates but also those with their bosses. These studies show as well that this aspect of management, essential though it is to survival and advancement, is sometimes ignored by otherwise talented and aggressive managers. Indeed, some managers who actively and effectively supervise subordinates, products, markets, and technologies, nevertheless assume an almost passively reactive stance vis-a-vis their bosses. Such a stance practically always hurts these managers and their companies.

Ways of Managing your Leader

You must have a good understanding of the other person and yourself, especially regarding strengths, weaknesses, work styles, and needs. You must use this information to develop and manage a healthy working relationship—one that is compatible with both persons' work styles assets, is characterized by mutual expectations, and meets the most critical needs of the other person. That is essentially what we have found highly effective managers doing.

Managing your boss requires that you gain an understanding of both the boss and his context as well as your own situation and needs. All managers do this to some degree, but many are not thorough enough. At a minimum, the manager needs to appreciate the boss' goals, and pressures, his or her strengths and weaknesses. Does he or she like to get information through memos, formal meetings, or phone calls? Does the boss thrive on conflict or try to minimize it?

The manager must be alert for opportunities to question the boss and others around him or her to test their assumptions. He should also pay attention to clues in the boss' behaviour. Although it is imperative that they do this when they begin working with a new boss, effective managers also continue to do this because they recognize that priorities and concerns change.

The manager should become keenly aware of what it is about himself that impedes or facilitates working with his boss and, with that awareness, take actions that make the relationship more effective.

Without this information, a manager is flying blind when dealing with his boss, and unnecessary conflicts, misunderstandings, and problems are inevitable.

According to Jan Mayer-Rodriguez

> *"Managing your boss isn't a matter of "apple polishing" or playing politics. It involves working together to generate the best solutions for you, your boss and your company"*

Can we really manage who we work for? Probably not, but we can enhance our relationship with them by effective communication, better understanding of their preferred leadership style, and by building an open and trusting relationship.

We should start by aligning expectations and having clear organizational vision and mission statements, with supporting goals; we must know our responsibilities and how we support attaining shared goals, and hold one another accountable for our actions (or lack of actions).

Joe Takash and Bahaudin Mujtaba, management experts, provide the following 8 tips to improve the boss relationship:

Learn the boss' communication style

What level of detail do they prefer? How often do they want to meet? Identify who seems to communicate best with them and try incorporating their style with yours.

Be proactive

Understand the strengths you bring to the organization and ensure that the boss is aware of them. If you have ideas, share them and be prepared with a plan to start to take action.

Meet regularly

Schedule (minimally) monthly meetings; discuss progress against goals, identify areas for improvement, and incorporate the results into your development plan.

Ask for the boss' opinion

Ask for their perspective on things. State your idea and approach and ask for their input. If you are the boss, ask your team for their ideas and *listen*.

Go to the boss with solutions

Most of us have heard "don't come to me with problems, come to me with solutions". That does not mean that we do not ask for help or have questions, but rather that we have thought it through, have solutions (which may have failed) but would now like another opinion.

Develop a power that makes you attractive

Become an expert, stay abreast of changes in your industry, understand the competition, have the dream customer/business partner relationship.

Address problems

If you seem at odds with the boss, talk to him or her. Do it when you can have one another's full attention, remain fact-based as to why you feel uncomfortable, and keep your emotions in check.

Play devil's advocate

This does not mean having open disagreements or making the boss look "wrong". Instead say "Let me play devil's advocate" so you are viewed as stating an alternate opinion which may bring additional light to the situation.

Invest the time to build a relationship with the boss, understand how they prefer to be communicated with, and model your leadership behaviours to support those preferences.

Chapter Nine

DEVELOPING AND MANAGING THE BOSS-SUBORDINATE RELATIONSHIP

COMPATIBLE WORK STYLES

Above all, a good working relationship with a boss accommodates differences in work style. Subordinates can adjust their styles in response to their boss' preferred method for receiving information. Peter Drucker divides bosses into "listeners" and "readers." Some bosses like to get information in report form so that they can read and study it. Others work better with information and reports presented in person so that they can ask questions. As Drucker points out, the implications are obvious. If your boss is a listener, you brief him or her in person, *and then* follow it up with a memo. If your boss is a reader, you cover important items or proposals in a memo or report, *and then* discuss them with him or her.

Other adjustments can be made according to a boss' decision-making style. Some bosses prefer to be involved in decisions and problems as they arise. These are high-involvement managers who like to keep their hands on the pulse of the operation. Usually their needs (and your own) are best satisfied if you touch base with them whenever necessary. A boss who has a need to be involved will become involved one way or another, so there are advantages in including him or her at your initiative. Other bosses prefer to delegate; they do not want to be involved. They expect you to come to them with major problems and inform them of important changes. Creating a compatible relationship also involves drawing on each other's strengths and making up for each other's weaknesses.

MUTUAL EXPECTATIONS

The subordinate who passively assumes that he or she knows what the boss expects is in for trouble. Of course, some superiors will spell out their expectations very explicitly and in great detail. But most do not. And although many corporations have systems that provide a basis for communicating expectations (such as formal planning processes, career planning reviews, and performance appraisal reviews), these systems never work perfectly. Also, between these formal reviews, expectations invariably change.

Ultimately, the burden falls on the subordinate to find out what the boss' expectations are. These expectations can be both broad (regarding, for example, what kinds of problems the boss wishes to be informed about and when) as well as very specific (regarding such things as when a particular project should be completed and what kinds of information the boss needs in the interim).

Developing a workable set of mutual expectations also requires that you communicate your own expectations to the boss, find out if they are realistic, and influence the boss to accept the ones that are important to you. Being able to influence the boss to value your expectations can be particularly important if the boss is an over-achiever. Such a boss will often set unrealistically high standards that need to be brought into line with reality.

A FLOW OF INFORMATION

How much information a boss needs about what a subordinate is doing will vary significantly depending on the boss' style, the situation the boss is in, and the confidence the boss has in the subordinate. But it is not uncommon for a boss to need more information than the subordinate would naturally supply or for the subordinate to think the boss knows more than he or she really does. Effective managers recognize that they probably underestimate what the boss needs to know and make sure they find ways to keep the boss informed through a process that fits his or her style.

Managing the flow of information upward is particularly difficult if the boss does not like to hear about problems. Although many would deny it, bosses often give off signals that they want to hear only good news. They show great displeasure—usually non-verbally—when someone tells them about a problem. Ignoring individual achievement, they may even evaluate more favourably subordinates who do not bring problems to them.

Nevertheless, for the good of the organization, boss and subordinate, a superior should hear about failures as well as successes. Some subordinates deal with a good-news-only boss by finding indirect ways to get the necessary information to him. Others see to it that potential problems, whether in the form of good surprises or bad news, are communicated immediately.

DEPENDABILITY AND HONESTY

Few things are more disabling to bosses than subordinates on whom they cannot depend, whose work they cannot trust. I believe no one is intentionally undependable, but many managers are inadvertently so because of oversight or uncertainty about the boss' priorities. A commitment to an optimistic delivery date may please a superior in the short term but be a source of displeasure if not honoured. It is difficult for a boss to rely on a subordinate who repeatedly slips deadlines.

It is almost impossible for bosses to work effectively if they cannot rely on a fairly accurate reading from their subordinates. Because it undermines credibility, dishonesty is perhaps the most troubling trait a subordinate can exhibit. Without a basic level of trust in a subordinate's word, a boss feels constrained to check all of a subordinate's decisions, which makes it difficult to delegate.

GOOD USE OF TIME AND RESOURCES

Your boss is probably as limited in his or her store of time, energy, and influence as you are. Every request you make of your boss uses up some of these resources. For this reason, common sense suggests drawing on these resources with some selectivity. This may sound obvious, but it is surprising how many managers use up their boss' time (and some of their own credibility) over relatively trivial issues.

In conclusion

As the world shrinks smaller and smaller into what we now see as a global village in which recruiters and head hunters scramble for human resources across several frontiers, it is now imperative, more than ever before, for organisations and even individuals that want to excel, to appreciate how culturally diverse our workplace has become, and adjust to it.

International job fairs are now part of HR manager's job. According to BBC news, ethnic minorities are set to make up one fifth of UK's population by 2015 and we already are seeing the rapidly changing demographic within the UK workforce. A few years ago, it would have been unimaginable that a foreigner could be appointed to the most senior position in the Bank of England; but on November 26, 2012, the British Chancellor, George Osborne, announced the appointment of Canadian Mark Joseph Carney as the new Governor of the Bank of England.

A reporting individuals that wants to lead from bottom up has to constantly have at the back of his or her mind that the leader 'does not always know better than the subordinate about everything' and might try to cover up by taking up the role of the questioner.

One great tool that can help the reporting manager or individuals guard against conflict with the boss is **Transactional Analysis**.

Transactional Analysis is a model that helps us understand why people think and act the way they do. It looks at a person's internal state and how it influences behaviour.

Irrespective of our social status, nationality or gender, all operate in three ego states, and each of them can be activated at an appropriate time. An awareness of Transactional Analysis will help both the superior and subordinate become more effective in their interpersonal skills.

Understanding the ego state the boss is at any particular time will help the subordinate identify and assume the complimentary state which will forestall potential conflict.

REFERENCES

1. Napoleon Hill, You Can Work Your Own Miracles, Napoleon Hill Foundation, 1971.
2. Emma S. Etuk, Recipe for Success: The 21 Indispensable Things that can help you Succeed in Life, 2004.
3. Alan Nelson, & Stan Toler, The 5 secrets to becoming a leader, Matthew Christian Publication, 2002.
4. Napoleon Hill, Think and Grow Rich, Ballantine Books, 1960.
5. John Adair, Adair on Leadership, Thorogood publishing. London: 2004.
6. Dave Buchanan and Richard Badham, Power, Politics, and Organizational Change. 1999, Saga Publications, London.
7. John Sparrow; Knowledge in Organizations: 1998, Sage Publications: London.
8. Samuel S.O. Afemikhe; the Pursuit of Value for Money: 2003, Spectrum Books Limited, Ibadan, Nigeria.
9. Francis C. Wilkinson and Linda K. Lewis, 2003, Greenwood Publishing Group, U.S.A
10. http://www.cvtips.com/career_advice_forum/-vp9652. html#9652